Tropical Ghana *Delights*

Tropical Ghana

Foods that will make your love interest go "mmm!"

Delights

CHARLES A. CANN

Notice

Mention of specific brands, companies, organizations, or authorities in this book does not imply endorsement by the author
or publisher, nor does mention of specific brands, companies, organizations, or authorities imply that they endorse this book,
its author, or the publisher.

The recipes contained in this book are to be followed exactly as written.
The publisher is not responsible for your specific health or allergy needs that may require medical supervision.
The publisher is not responsible for any adverse reactions to the recipes contained in this book.

Internet addresses and telephone numbers given in this book were accurate at the time it went to press.
Neither the author nor publisher assume responsibility for errors, or for changes that occur after publication.

Printed in the United States of America
First Printing

ISBN: 978-0-6151-7155-5

Written by: Charles A. Cann
Editor: Nicole L. Joseph
Layout & Design: Tiffany Sakato
Photography: Thomas Lee
Cartoon Art: Miguel Jiron

For more information, visit www.lulu.com

For you, Mama Kate,
for making me
a marvelous cook
and a tropical Ghana chef

SPECIAL THANKS

To Mama Kate, for the discipline, joy and love you taught me in working with food and life. To my family, for cooking all the time and thinking I was joking when I said I would publish a cookbook. To my mother, for always cooking too much, and we still never ate enough for you. To my aunts, Esther and Mavis, who made me bake whenever I was in London and to Aunt Doris for your suggestions.

To Nicole Joseph for agreeing to work with me as editor, Thomas Lee for the photo shoots, Tiffany Sakato for the layout and for telling everyone about my cooking, Miguel Jiron for your cartoon art, Mabel Ntiru for taking time to review my book and for all your suggestions and to Cynthia and Lynn for enjoying and raving about my cooking. To Saul, Peter and Pat for loving Ghanaian food, Win-Sie for letting me know it is important to include options for vegetarians and to Angela and Andy for talking about my cooking all the time. To Osato, your special help is very much appreciated.

To Rev. Festus Johnson for inspiring my life and for all your prayers and to Linda Kolbusz for having a special place in your heart for me and for your help. To the Lavidas, especially Mrs. Lavidas for talking about food whenever I stopped by your home. To John, Michelle and Cary for all your help in finding that one ingredient. To Elizabeth, for your love for food and for trying my recipes without complaints.

To everyone who gave me their honest opinions after sampling my food. And to all my many friends, who continue to show their loving support.

Contents

Introduction

WHY *TROPICAL GHANA DELIGHTS*?

My family and friends have questioned why this cookbook is called "Tropical Ghana Delights." First and foremost, I employed "Tropical" because I use tropical ingredients. All the recipes in this book can be prepared in any tropical region as well as anywhere you can find tropical ingredients in the world – whether in New York, Miami, England, India, Tokyo, Australia, Jamaica or Ghana. I use "Ghana" in the title because it is where I grew up, developed my cooking talent and draw all my inspiration and influence. My inclusion of "Delights" in the title is a way of saying the recipes are original, exquisite, fruit infused and satisfying.

Additionally, when I conceived the idea of a cookbook, the idea was to concentrate mainly on hors d'oeuvres – fingers foods which I called "delights" because they melt in your mouth and strike a new chord in you. "Tropical Ghana Delights" is a simple and affordable way to experience the tropics – blend in spices, add fresh flavor and heat up your kitchen anytime.

FRUIT INFUSED

I love fruits so much that I have discovered ways to infuse fruits into everything that goes in my stomach. I believe my love for fruits developed in Ghana, where I grew up on a farmhouse with a lot of different fruit trees – three mango trees, 20 coconut trees, a soursop tree, sweetsop, cashew, guava, tangerine, and so many more which I loved for both their beauty and their taste.

Because of this special love, you will find that most of my recipes include some of my favorite fruits like tangerines, pineapples and mangos. Of course, my love for carrots (which I eat daily), tomatoes, basil, ginger, onions, sweet potatoes, avocados and honey will also be very evident.

FRESHNESS & LEFTOVERS

Because of my upbringing as a farmer and my daily use of fresh produce from the garden, I restrict my ingredients to mostly fresh foods. I use very little canned or processed food. I encourage this because it makes foods taste better, makes it healthier and it brings out the tropical flavors. Because I had a lot of farm produce easily within my reach, fresh food has become part of my life. And in order to enjoy the recipes in this book, please try to do the same.

Another blessing in my life is that my mother raised me to never waste food. So whenever there was leftover food we would find a way to repackage it in a different way. Many of the recipes in this book are linked to each other. For example, with the remains from the Painted Fish, you can start the Plantain Boats recipe. You can use bread slices you think are almost old to make something new. You leave them in the oven over low heat and crush them to use as breadcrumbs; it tastes better and fresher than packaged breadcrumbs on store shelves. I use only homemade breadcrumbs. There is no better way to save money, avoid wasting and enjoy your food as fresh as possible.

INSPIRED FROM ABOVE

The recipes in this book are original with the exception of a few remixed recipes developed from when my mother taught me to cook during my childhood in Ghana. My friends always want to know how I get these ideas. I call it the "process." The "process" is a blessing from God. I go to sleep, and God inspires my food dreams. When I wake up, I know the specific tropical ingredients that I need to use and how to combine them. Sometimes the dream might not be clear, but as I pray during my morning quiet time with God, I get a revelation on how to combine the ingredients. Some of the ingredients are left over from previous cooking sessions, so I wake up and get the idea to add something else to them to make a new recipe, rather than waste them.

With the "process," I cannot speed it or change it – I just let it be. To make this process complete, I added a 3-step approval process. I prepare a dish based on my inspired dream, try it out myself, and then find ways of improving the taste. After these changes – whether they are additions or subtractions – I invite friends to try it and give me their thoughts. Based on my friends' critiques, I make a few more changes, then have another friend try it, completing the 3-step approval process.

MARVELOUS COOK? BECAUSE I LOVE FOOD

I love my poem (dedication) that talks about me being a "marvelous cook." I do not have a food preparation certificate, but I have gained the most amazing experience over the past years. My entire family cooks, so for me to cook is no surprise. But I think the content of this book was born from the days I awoke to the sweet aroma of oven fresh baked bread (Ghana style) from our home bakery, an aroma that filled the neighborhood before the cock crowed. The aroma sometimes lingered overnight, especially during special occasions and holidays. This aroma, an aroma so sweet that it mixed with the tropical heat perfectly, seemed to make life better because you would always look forward to a fresh plate of good food.

I did not realize how much those days would influence me until now. Mama Kate, a professional caterer, had a special touch on different foods that always drew neighbors and friends over to enjoy a hot meal. And for me, several years of growing up with my aunt, my mentor, my inspiration and enjoying these meals, assisting her with her work – watching, learning, measuring, tasting, preparing and, yes, burning a few baked foods here and there – made me her unofficial assistant and definitely a marvelous cook. Thank you, Mama Kate, for this blessing.

Tropical Guide

 – Meals that take no more than 30 minutes to cook

 – Special serving size (larger portions)

V – The recipe is vegetarian friendly, with a few simple changes

+ – You can add more ingredients at your discretion to make tastier or more colourful

4 oz (2 cups) – Measurement are made simple in both metric and imperial systems

Olive oil – Olive oil preferred but vegetable oil can be used as a substitute

M.I.N. – Make it Now

ON A LIGHT NOTE

Chicken-Shrimp Pseudo Soup, p. 6

Chicken-Shrimp Pseudo Soup

Serves: 5

 – 3 NYC taxi drivers

Prep Time: 10 minutes
Cooking Time: 25 minutes

As the name suggests, it is not a real soup. I was stir frying one day with whatever ingredients I could find at home. As I threw ingredient after ingredient in my wok, it turned out that I did not enjoy my stir fry in the end. But I did not waste it. I saved it for the next day. Luckily I was inspired through a dream on what to add to make it work. I went to grab the extra ingredients, but it still did not make the cut for me. Several days later, as I was praying, I had a revelation of what I needed to omit and add to make this fake soup "real." If you desire something light but inspiring, try this and enjoy its fakeness.

- 2 lbs (32oz) medium shrimp, cleaned and peeled
- 2 lbs (32oz) boneless chicken breast, cleaned and diced
- 1 tablespoon olive oil (or vegetable oil)
- 10 tablespoons water
- 5 tablespoons minced sun-dried tomatoes
- 3 tablespoons soy sauce
- 2 teaspoons black pepper
- 2 teaspoons seasoned salt (or salt)
- 10 scallions (or spring onions), cleaned and chopped
- 1 medium cauliflower, cleaned and chopped
- 1 medium red onion, cleaned and chopped
- 1 medium yellow onion, cleaned and chopped
- 1 teaspoon cayenne pepper
- 2 tablespoons worcestershire sauce
- 3 tablespoons cooking wine
- 1 teaspoon sugar
- 1 cup (8oz) fresh corn eyes (or grains) or 1 (12oz) can of drained sweet corn

M.I.N.

In a wok, toss shrimp with olive oil, 1 teaspoon seasoned salt and black pepper over medium heat until lightly cooked.

Pour shrimp onto a plate and toss diced chicken in wok, add remainder of seasoned salt and black pepper, stirring continuously for about 10 minutes. As chicken cooks, add sun-dried tomatoes and sugar. Continue stirring for another 5 minutes. Add all onions, and stir for another 2 minutes.

Add cooking wine, soy sauce, worcestershire sauce and cayenne pepper. Stir, toss shrimp back in and add cauliflower. Increase heat to high and stir for 3 – 5 minutes. Add corn and water.

Continue stirring for another 5 minutes, and you are ready to serve this on a light note.

Rice Salad V+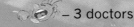

Serves: 5 — 3 doctors

Prep Time: 20 minutes
Cooking Time: 15 minutes

• 1 cup steamed rice
• 1 lb (16oz) ham (or your favorite deli meat)
• 2 large ripe mangoes
• 1 hard ripe papaya (or pawpaw)
• 1 large carrot
• ½ cup (4oz) evaporated milk

Tip #1: Ditch The Ham!
Replace ham with tofu for a vegetarian option.

Tip #2: More Meat!
Add two or more kinds of deli meats to make it tastier.

M.I.N.

Cut ham or deli meat into ½ inch by ½ inch cubes and place in a serving bowl.

Peel mango and cut into 1 inch by ½ inch strips; place in a separate serving bowl.

Peel, seed and cut papaya (pawpaw) into ½ inch by ½ inch cubes and place in a serving bowl.

Clean and cut carrot into 1 inch by ½ inch strips and place in a serving bowl.

In a salad plate serve yourself about 3 tablespoons of steamed rice, 6 each of ham, mango, papaya and carrot, and top it with 2 tablespoons evaporated milk or your favorite salad dressing. Enjoy the rice salad on a light note while relaxing in your chair.

This recipe started as a salad and turned into more of a finger food. But based on feedback from my friends who are always willing to sample and let me know what to change, it has returned to its original form as a salad. When you first hear the name, it makes you think that you can make a salad out of anything these days; maybe you can, but this has its own tropical feel that makes it amazing. Should you want to go to the beach for a picnic, think of including this recipe in your cooler and enjoy the warmth of the beach while you chill with some cool Rice Salad.

Tropical Special Salad +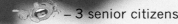

Serves: 5 – 3 senior citizens

Prep Time: 20 minutes / Cooking Time: 10 minutes

• 2 fresh farm grilled white corn (or maize), taken off cob
or 1 (12oz) can of drained sweet corn
• 2 cups (16oz) fresh cleaned lettuce tossed with white vinegar
• 1 medium cucumber seeded and diced
• 2 medium carrots chopped into 1 inch rectangles
• 2 scallions (or spring onions), chopped and tossed with white vinegar
• ½ cup (4oz) finely chopped cabbage tossed with white vinegar
• 1 large ripe mango chopped into 1 inch rectangles
• ½ medium pineapple, peeled and diced
• 1½ lb boneless chicken breast tossed with seasoned salt and 1 tablespoon olive oil, grilled and cut into 1 inch strips
• 2 lbs cleaned medium shrimp spiced with seasoned salt and tossed with 2 tablespoons olive oil in pan over medium heat until cooked
• 3 avocados, diced

M.I.N.

Set all the ingredients in different sized bowls that accommodate each amount.

On a salad plate, put lettuce on the bottom and toss in other ingredients. Top the salad with chicken, shrimp and avocado (in that order).

Enjoy the salad with or without your favorite dressing.

Tip: Keep It Alive!

Combine ingredients just before serving, and toss avocado with lemon juice to prevent discoloring.

This salad is special because the ingredients bring out a lot of tropical colors – hence its name, Tropical Special Salad. The salad has just about everything you can think of that you can find in any tropical region in the world. The salad started as a simple combination of ingredients and they kept growing in number until the perfect mix was created. It tastes better, fresher and more tropical when you combine the ingredients just before serving it. Eat it as is or add your favorite salad dressing, and enjoy the fresh flavor of vegetables, fruits and meat combined specially for you when you want to eat something on a light note.

Grandmama Light Soup

Serves: 6 – 4 mothers

Prep Time: 30 minutes / Cooking Time: 90 minutes

Light Soup is a tomato based soup popular in Ghana and eaten with fufu. It is the soup I was fed whenever I felt feverish, caught a cold or felt sick. It always did the trick as it is very nutritious. Many of my friends and other people I have met almost always say their grandmother's cooking is the best, and I agree with them. So I figured if my grandmama and many other "grandmamas" make such lasting food impressions, I need to honor them. And knowing that I always wanted "more" in my soup when I was sick so I could get all the nutrients to recover faster, I took this popular Ghanaian soup to a different level. I explored ways to make it more nutritious by adding more vegetables that will leave a lasting impression like grandmama's recipe. Though this recipe works on a light note, remember your grandmama's food and try it to revive your spirit not only when you are feverish, but to get a little healthy kick any day.

- 1 lb (16oz) beef, cut into small chunks
- 1 lb (16oz) goat meat, cleaned, cut to small chunks
- 10 tablespoons tomato paste (or puree)
- 6 large ripe tomatoes
- 2 large red onions
- 2 medium yellow onions
- 12 cups (96oz) water
- 3 cloves garlic
- 2 okro (okra)
- 1 medium carrot
- 1 medium eggplant (or aubergine)
- ½ medium cucumber, seeded
- 1 green habanero pepper
- ¼ head of cauliflower
- ½ cup (4oz) fresh basil leaves
- 3 teaspoons white pepper
- 2 teaspoons black pepper
- 2 tablespoons salt
- 4 bay leaves
- 1 teaspoon curry powder
- 2 large peeled pieces ginger root
- 3 tablespoons worcestershire sauce

M.I.N.

Place beef and goat meat in large soup pot over medium heat. Finely chop one red onion and add to meat. Add white and black peppers, curry and worcestershire sauce and stir continuously for about 10 minutes as meats steam fries.

Partly cover pot for another 10 minutes as meats continue to steam, stirring occasionally.

Wash and clean all vegetables and add tomatoes, onions, garlic cloves, one ginger root, okro, eggplant, cucumber, habanero pepper and bay leaves; cover pot completely and let steam for about 5 minutes.

Add 6 cups of water and increase heat to high. Allow vegetables to cook (about 20 – 25 minutes).

Pick out all the vegetables and divide into 2 parts in order to blend. Add 3 cups water to each part and blend completely. Pour blender vegetable mix through a colander over boiling meat.

Add salt and tomato paste and let boil for 30 minutes.

In a small pot, steam cauliflower. Add any remaining cauliflower stock to the soup.

Finely chop the remaining ginger root and add to soup. Finely chop basil leaves and add. Reduce heat to medium and let boil for another 20 – 30 minutes.

Serve this in a soup bowl on a light note by topping with steamed cauliflower.

FINGER FOODS
(HORS D'OEUVRES)

Honey Green Chicken, p. 11

Honey Green Chicken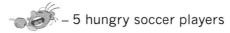

Serves: 10

– 5 hungry soccer players

Prep Time: 3 hours (for chicken marinade)
Cooking Time: 20 minutes

Honey Green Chicken started this cook book. It has undergone many transformations in the last five years, making it my oldest recipe. I cannot remember exactly how it started, but I believe it was just a simple chicken recipe made with scallions to give it its green color. However it only turned out great after I was blessed with the exact vision of how to make it superb. Honey Green Chicken strikes a cord that leaves every chicken lover asking for more. Honey Green Chicken also makes a perfect recipe to get a love interest thinking of committing to a more exclusive relationship.

• 3 lbs (48oz) thinly sliced boneless chicken breast

For Marinade

• 2 tablespoons olive oil (or vegetable oil)
• 2 tablespoons worcestershire sauce
• 1 tablespoon freshly minced ginger root
• 1 tablespoon freshly minced garlic (or 2 cloves)
• 1 teaspoon seasoned salt (or salt)
• 1 teaspoon white pepper

For Green Syrup

• 4 tablespoons honey
• 5 tablespoons mayonnaise
• 4 cleaned chopped scallions (or spring onions)
• ½ small chopped red onion
• ½ small chopped yellow onion
• 6 tablespoons finely chopped basil (or 3 sprigs)
• 1 lemon
• 1 tangerine

M.I.N.

Combine ingredients for marinade and mix completely. Place chicken in bowl and pour marinade on top. Cover and place in fridge for 3 hours or overnight.

Blend all onions and 4 tablespoons of the basil with tangerine juice. Add honey and mayonnaise. Grate in lemon rind. Squeeze in lemon juice from half of the lemon. Mix completely.

Preheat grill to medium heat.

Take chicken out of fridge and place pieces one at a time into the green syrup in a large bowl, coating well. Grill chicken pieces until lightly green with golden brown spots.

Place cooked chicken on a chopping board and sprinkle with remaining basil. Cut chicken in strips, place on serving plate and stick toothpicks in strips to serve this "chicken-lovers favorite" recipe.

Mackerel Tarts

Serves: 20 – 10 party crashers

Prep Time: 30 minutes
Cooking Time: 15 minutes

Mackerel Tarts is a recipe I like to refer to as a leftover recipe. It was born one day after I finished making Honey Green Chicken and I still had some green syrup left. I figured since I also had some leftover grilled mackerel, I should make something new and different. I was not sure if it would work out well. And now I have christened the Mackerel Tart as a new recipe of the Tropical Ghana Delights. Mackerel lovers will know what I mean when they try this out and dip it in ketchup. It is a definite "must-try" and tastes fruity when you use pineapple jam as your dip.

Tip: Fish More!
Replace mackeral with your favorite type of fish.

- 1 medium salted, grilled mackerel
- 2 cups (16oz) breadcrumbs
- 4 tablespoons honey
- 5 tablespoons mayonnaise
- 3 cleaned chopped scallions (spring onions)
- ½ small chopped red onion
- ½ small chopped yellow onion
- 6 tablespoons fresh basil (or 3 sprigs), finely chopped
- ½ teaspoon black pepper
- ½ teaspoon cayenne pepper
- 1 fresh lemon

Dip
- 4 tablespoons ketchup or
5 tablespoons pineapple jam (marmalade)
- 1 tangerine

M.I.N.
Blend all onions and basil. Add honey and mayonnaise. Grate in lemon rind and add lemon juice from half of the lemon. Mix completely.

Preheat oven to 450°F (232°C).

Skin grilled mackerel and remove bones. Flake the fish and add to basil mix, completely mixing it in. Add breadcrumbs gradually until mixture becomes solid.

Grease a baking sheet, and scoop 1 tablespoon full each for the tarts.

Place in oven for 5 minutes then reduce heat to 375°F (191°C); and let bake slowly for 10 minutes turning occasionally.

Serve this finger food with ketchup dip or tangerine juice mixed with pineapple jam (marmalade) dip.

Jumbo Fruity Shrimp

Serves: 5 — 2 bus drivers

Prep Time: 5 minutes / Cooking Time: 15 minutes

I love the name Jumbo Fruity Shrimp, and the name existed even before the recipe came to life. The original recipe had soursop (guanabana), but I had to omit this ingredient because it is hard to find. However the recipe, after all its changes, is still fruity and contains a special new delightful taste. "Would you Jumbo Fruity Shrimp?" Maybe you should give this finger food that is unique and fruity a try.

- 1 lb (16oz) jumbo shrimp, cleaned and peeled
- ½ cup breadcrumbs (homemade, 6 bread slices, grilled and crumbed)
- 2 tangerines
- ½ large ripe mango
- ¼ peeled sweet pineapple
- 1 lemon
- 3 tablespoons pineapple jam (or marmalade)
- 1 tablespoon olive oil (or vegetable oil)

M.I.N.

Combine tangerine juice, pineapple and mango in blender. Blend into fruit paste.

Set aside about half of the paste to use as dipping sauce.

Mix few drops of lemon juice with pineapple jam and coat shrimp.

Preheat grill to high.

Coat with fruit paste, and then sprinkle with breadcrumbs. Drizzle coated shrimp with olive oil and grill. Turn occasionally till cooked or golden orange.

Serve this finger food with remaining fruit paste as dipping sauce.

Plantain Boats V+

Serves: 20 – 10 birthday kids

Prep Time: 5 minutes
Cooking Time: 15 minutes

I love plantains, and I love them grilled. Growing up in Ghana gave me the opportunity to enjoy plantains on the street corner grills or at home. A few years ago, I remembered a childhood story which occurred while I was visiting a friend. My friend ate plantains like banana and fried bananas as plantain; "well they are from the same family," she suggested. Not long after recalling this story, I started dreaming about plantains in many more ways. Before I could ask myself "are you in love with plantains?" this recipe was born. Plantain Boats is one of the top three recipes in this book that takes you to a different level. Just remember not to miss the delightful unique taste as it melts in your mouth!

Tip: Ditch the Fish!
Omit fish to enjoy this dish vegetarian style.

• 5 large hard ripe plantains

For Boat Crew
• 1 teaspoon honey
• 1 medium finely chopped carrot
• ¼ medium red onion, finely chopped
• ¼ medium yellow onion, finely chopped
• 1 finely chopped scallion (or spring onion)
• ¼ medium green pepper, finely chopped
• ¼ medium red pepper, finely chopped
• ¼ medium yellow pepper, finely chopped
• ½ teaspoon freshly minced ginger root
• 1 tablespoon lemon juice
• 2 avocados, sliced
• 5 tablespoons flaked skinless grilled fish (or drained tuna flakes)

• 2 tablespoons orange or pineapple jam (or marmalade)

M.I.N.
Preheat grill to medium heat.

Peel skin off plantains. Cut each plantain along the length into two. Then cut each slice in half again, creating quarters. With a potato peeler or small knife, carve out the seeds to create an opening for the boat crew.

Place plantains on grill, flipping occasionally until light brown or cooked. As plantain grills, make a colorful crew by mixing all the vegetables together with the minced ginger, lemon juice and honey.

As plantain comes off grill, place on a plate. Put in 1 – 2 teaspoons of fish flakes as seats for boat crew. Fill rest of plantain opening with vegetable mix. Top with half a teaspoon pineapple jam, and place avocado slices flat on top as boat sails. Serve this finger food hot right from the grill.

Plantain Mama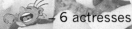

Serves: 12 — 6 actresses

Prep Time: 5 minutes / Cooking Time: 30 minutes

Plantain Mama! "Something for Mama, too?" This recipe is dedicated to all the "Mamas" who keep toiling to make life easy for me and you. Plantain Mama is the last recipe to make it in before publishing. Just when you keep wondering – "what else can I do with plantains?" – now you can surprise everyone with this simple but wonderful recipe. Don't wait till Mother's Day! Make it a delightful day for your mother right now!

Tip: Cheese It or Make It Fruity!
Top Plantain Mama with grated Edam cheese or your favorite fruits.

• ½ lb (8oz) fresh beef sirloin, cleaned and cut into thin 1-inch strips

For Marinade
• 2 tablespoons olive oil (vegetable oil)
• 1 tablespoon worcestershire sauce
• 1 tablespoon white vinegar
• 1 teaspoon seasoned salt (or salt)
• 1 teaspoon black pepper

Plantain Bread
• 4 soft ripe plantains, peeled
• 1 cup (8oz) all purpose flour
• ½ teaspoon cayenne pepper
• 1 teaspoon baking powder

• 2 scallions (or spring onions), cleaned and finely chopped
• ½ medium carrot, finely chopped
• 1 small red onion, finely chopped
• ½ of medium green pepper, finely chopped
• 1 teaspoon freshly minced ginger root
• 1 teaspoon freshly minced garlic (1 clove)
• 1 medium hard ripe mango
• 1 teaspoon black pepper
• 1 teaspoon freshly minced basil
• 1 teaspoon soy sauce
• 1 tablespoon brandy
• 2 tablespoons cooking wine

M.I.N.

Combine ingredients for marinade and mix completely with beef. Stir-fry in wok over high heat for about 10 – 15 minutes until beef stock starts simmering.

Add ginger, garlic, basil, curry powder, black pepper and scallions as beef starts sizzling. Continue stirring and add brandy, cooking wine and soy sauce. Let sizzle for 2 minutes.

Let cool for a minute then mix in mango, green pepper, carrots and red onion.

Preheat oven grill and cut 2 sheets (about 8-inches by 12-inches) of aluminum foil.

Peel plantains into a bowl and mash it with potato masher. Add flour, baking powder and cayenne pepper and mix completely.

Place 1 sheet foil on a flat baking sheet and pour plantain bread mix onto it. Use a spatula to spread mix on the foil. Place in oven grill and let grill for 8 – 10 minutes until golden brown.

With second sheet of foil on golden brown side, flip plantain bread. Peel foil off the back and let the other side grill till golden brown.

Remove from grill and cut plantain bread into 12 pieces. Top each piece with a tablespoon of beef mix and serve this finger food hot for Mama.

Bacon Basil Wrap +

Serves: 10 – 5 teachers

Prep Time: 10 minutes / Cooking Time: 30 minutes

Bacon! We all know it's very tasty (especially if you are a bacon lover like me). However, it tastes even better when added to another ingredient. Bacon Basil Wrap makes bacon taste better and gives you an additional basil flavor. I discovered this recipe when I had too much batata (sweet potato) in my food stock. I combined it with bacon and "mmm, mmm, mmm," I knew it. One morning I realized that basil was what I needed to make this recipe taste better, not just better but "tropical freshness" better. You cannot serve your cocktail guests without bacon basil wraps because not only is it quick and easy to prepare, but it has a fruity dip that will keep everyone looking out for the serving tray.

- 20 slices of bacon
- 20 fresh basil leaves
- 2 large batata (or sweet potato)
- 3 sweet tangerines
- 1 large ripe mango
- 1 cup (8oz) water
- ¼ cup (2oz) evaporated milk

Dip

Blend mango with tangerine juice to create a mango-tangerine dip. Replace toothpicks with new ones if burned in oven and serve this finger food with this special dip.

Tip: Enjoy Your Favorite!
Replace bacon with slices of your favorite deli meat.

M.I.N.

Peel and cut batata into 3 inch by ½ inch long strips. Place in a cooking pot over high heat and add 1 cup water. Bring to boil for about 12 – 15 minutes or until almost cooked. Drain water.

Preheat oven to 450°F (232°C).

Wrap each piece of batata with a leaf of basil, followed by a slice of bacon. Wrap bacon completely around batata. Hold bacon in place with toothpicks. Brush with milk.

Place in oven for 10 minutes then reduce heat to 375°F (191°C) and let bake slowly for 10 – 15 minutes, turning occasionally.

Egg Plates +

Serves: 8 — 4 hungry farmers

Prep Time: 10 minutes / Cooking Time: 30 minutes

The story behind the Egg Plate is probably the funniest. I loved eggs as a kid (occasionally played with them, even though I did not break any) but for some reason, I have minimized my egg intake over the years. Sometimes I go to the grocery store, and when I get to the eggs section, I stare for a long time wasting precious minutes – wondering whether to buy a dozen or more or less. Eventually I leave without getting any eggs. So I started thinking of other ways I could use eggs than just the familiar ways.

After several months, it dawned on me that an egg plate might be the answer. Originally called White Egg Plate, I realized it needed color to bring out the tropical spirit. And adding avocado to it makes it just the right finger food delight.

- 1 dozen eggs
- 1 tablespoon salt
- 3½ cups (28oz) water
- 2 tablespoons butter
- 1 tablespoon honey
- 4 tablespoons mayonnaise
- 1 medium yuca (or cassava), peeled and cleaned
- 1 medium batata (or sweet potatoes), peeled and cleaned
- 1 medium yautia (or cocoyam), peeled and cleaned
- 1 medium West African yam, (or potato) peeled and cleaned

Make It Colourful
- 1 avocado
- 1 small carrot
- 1 green pepper
- 1 red pepper
- 1 yellow pepper
- 1 scallion (spring onion)

M.I.N.

Boil eggs with 2½ cups (20oz) water and salt for about 20 – 25 minutes over medium heat.

Cut yuca, batata, yautia and potato into pieces, and boil with remaining water over high heat for about 20 minutes. Drain water. Mash the mixture into smooth, lump-free paste and add in butter, honey and mayonnaise. Mix well.

Place cooked eggs in cold water for 5 minutes. Remove shells and cut into halves along the length, discarding the yolk.

Place eggs on a plate. Put potato mix in a piping bag, select your favorite tip and pipe the filling into each egg half, filling completely the hole created by the yolk.

Make this finger food a delight by garnishing the egg tops with finely chopped carrots, green, red or yellow peppers or scallions. Or try topping with slices of avocado.

Tangerine Ginger Chicken

Tangerine Ginger Chicken was originally only for my cookbook website, but its popularity soared so I had to include it in the book. Many friends who tried it rave about the tangerine flavor. This recipe started on a rainy day when I did not want to go to the store. I figured I should stay dry and use my ginger root, tangerine and chicken to make a good meal. And several more rainy days later, here we are with a final recipe that can save you on a rainy day with some delicious tangerine flavor.

Serves: 5 — 5 starving artists

Prep Time: 15 minutes / Cooking Time: 10 minutes

• 1½ lbs (24oz) cleaned thinly sliced chicken breast

For Marinade
• 2 tablespoons olive oil
• 1 tablespoon worcestershire sauce
• 2 teaspoons fresh minced garlic
• 1 teaspoon salt
• ½ teaspoon cayenne pepper

For Tangerine Ginger Mix
• 6 large sweet tangerines
• 1 large cleaned ginger root

M.I.N.
Combine ingredients for marinade and pour over chicken in a bowl. Cover and refrigerate for 10 minutes.

Cut ginger in pieces and combine with three juiced tangerines in a blender. Preheat grill or grilling pan.

Pour tangerine ginger mix over chicken, and coat well. Grill chicken, turning occasionally till cooked, juicy and golden brown.

Peel and slice remaining tangerines, remove seeds and place over chicken.

Cut chicken into strips, stick toothpicks through tangerine slices and chicken, and serve this finger food as a Tropical Ghana Delight.

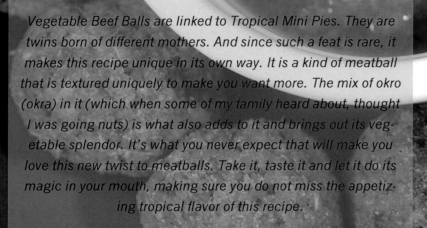

Vegetable Beef Balls are linked to Tropical Mini Pies. They are twins born of different mothers. And since such a feat is rare, it makes this recipe unique in its own way. It is a kind of meatball that is textured uniquely to make you want more. The mix of okro (okra) in it (which when some of my family heard about, thought I was going nuts) is what also adds to it and brings out its vegetable splendor. It's what you never expect that will make you love this new twist to meatballs. Take it, taste it and let it do its magic in your mouth, making sure you do not miss the appetizing tropical flavor of this recipe.

Vegetable Beef Balls, p. 21

I was inspired in less than 60 hours – yes that fast. I have worked with pies and pastries all my life, and I never understood why whenever I was in England, my Auntie Esther and Auntie Mavis would always make me bake them mini pies before I left, even if it was a very short visit. God had made it long before I knew, and I now know that I made my Aunties mini pies all that time to get ready for this recipe. That's what makes it very special. It has a unique blend of ingredients that gives it the exact tropical feel that will make you lick your fingers for more.

Tropical Mini Pies, p. 20

Tropical Mini Pies

Serves: 20 — a presidential team

Prep Time: 30 minutes / Cooking Time: 25 minutes

For Pastry

- 8 cups (64oz) all purpose flour
- 1¾ cup (14oz) margarine
- ½ cup (4oz) butter
- 1 teaspoon salt
- 1 teaspoon baking powder
- ½ cup (4oz) chilled water

For Filling

- ½ lb (8oz) fresh minced or ground beef sirloin
- 10 tablespoons sun-dried tomatoes
- 1 small okro (okra)
- ¼ of small white eggplant or aubergine
- 10 fresh basil leaves, cleaned and finely chopped
- 3 tablespoons freshly minced ginger root
- 2 scallions, cleaned and chopped
- 1 red onion, peeled and finely chopped
- 1 medium carrot, finely chopped
- 1 small batata (or sweet potato), peeled and finely chopped
- 1 small yautia (or cocoyam), peeled and finely chopped
- 1 teaspoon sugar
- 2 teaspoons black pepper
- 1 teaspoon white pepper
- 1 teaspoon curry powder
- 1 teaspoon salt
- ¾ cup (6oz) water
- 1 teaspoon butter
- ¼ cup (2oz) evaporated milk

M.I.N.

Mix flour, margarine and butter into a smooth pastry flour mix. Set aside 5 tablespoons pastry flour for rolling pastry later. Mix remainder with chilled water to create two big pastry balls. Place in fridge.

In a sauce pan, add 1 teaspoon butter to beef and steam over high heat for 7 minutes, or as beef changes from red to brown. Use a fork to flake beef as necessary to prevent lumps. Drain excess stock.

Boil sun-dried tomatoes with sugar and ¼ cup water over low heat until it starts simmering (about 10 minutes). Cut okra and eggplant into small pieces and boil with ½ cup water until tender. Drain remaining juice.

Add scallions to sun-dried tomato, okra and eggplant and blend into a smooth paste. Mix paste into steamed beef, add ginger, salt, white and black pepper. Mix well.

Add yautia, batata, basil, red onion and carrot, and mix well for a nice colorful pie filling mix.

With a rolling pin, roll out pastry close to ¼ inch thickness. Use a round cookie cutter (about 3½ inches in diameter) – or a circular object of similar size – to cut out pastry. Dip cutter in pastry flour and cut out round shapes. Fill each shape with about 1 teaspoon of pie filling.

Preheat oven to 450°F (232°C).

Brush the edges with water and fold over to create a moon shape. Press down the edges with your finger; the water on the edges makes it stick easily. Repeat until all pastry is used.

Use a fork to punch holes in the top of each piece of pie, and brush with milk before placing it in the oven.

Place in oven for 5 minutes; reduce heat to 375°F (191°C) and let bake slowly, turning occasionally for about 20 – 25 minutes, or until tops are golden brown.

Serve the finger food hot and let the tropical mini pie inspire you.

Vegetable Beef Balls

Serves: 25  – a swimming team

Prep Time: 30 minutes / Cooking Time: 25 minutes

- 1½ lbs (24oz) fresh minced beef sirloin
- 15 tablespoons sun-dried tomatoes
- 1 small okro (or okra)
- ¼ small white eggplant (or aubergine)
- 1 cup (8oz) fresh basil leaves, finely chopped
- 6 tablespoons fresh minced ginger root
- 4 scallions, cleaned and chopped
- 1 small batata (or sweet potato)
- 1 small yautia (or cocoyam)
- 1½ cups (12oz) fresh breadcrumbs
- 2 teaspoons sugar
- 2 teaspoons seasoned salt (or salt)
- 2 teaspoons curry powder
- 2 teaspoons black pepper
- 2 teaspoons white pepper
- 2 cups water

For Tomato Gravy Dip

- 2 tablespoons vegetable oil
- ¼ cup (2oz) water
- ½ teaspoon white pepper
- ½ teaspoon black pepper
- 1 teaspoon salt
- ½ teaspoon curry powder
- 1 teaspoon worcestershire sauce
- ½ teaspoon minced ginger

- ½ teaspoon minced garlic
- 2 tablespoons finely chopped basil
- 3 large ripe tomatoes
- 2 scallions (or spring onions)
- ½ small red onion, finely chopped
- 2 tablespoons tomato paste (or puree)

M.I.N.

Peel and cut yautia and batata into small cubes. Place in a large pot over high heat and add 1 cup water; boil for about 15 minutes or until cooked and tender. Drain water. Mash into lump-free paste.

Boil sun-dried tomatoes with sugar and ½ cup water over low heat until it starts simmering (about 10–15 minutes). Cut okra and eggplant into small pieces and boil with ½ cup water until tender.

Add scallions to sun-dried tomato, okra and eggplant, and blend into a smooth paste. Mix paste into minced beef, and add mashed batata variety mix, ginger, seasoned salt and white and black peppers. Mix all, and add finely chopped basil. Gradually stir in 1 cup breadcrumbs to the vegetable beef mix.

Preheat oven to 450°F (232°C).

Make medium ball shapes, using remaining breadcrumbs to help them form and place on greased baking sheet.

Place in oven for 5 minutes then reduce heat to 375°F (191°C) and let bake slowly, turning occasionally for 10 – 15 minutes. Let cool a little and serve the finger food warm.

For Dip (About 55 minutes)

In a saucepan combine oil, red onions, ginger and garlic over medium heat.

Blend scallions in blender. Add to sizzling garlic and ginger, and turn heat to high. Add tomato paste, and stir continuously for about 5 minutes. Add basil and continue stirring for 7 – 10 minutes.

Blend fresh tomatoes with water and add to gravy mix. Continue stirring for about 5 minutes. Partly cover with lid and let boil, stirring occasionally – about 15 minutes. Reduce heat to low and let boil gently for another 20 minutes, still stirring occasionally.

Tip: Time Saver!

Make sure to make dip as beef balls are cooking to save time.

Shrimp by Mango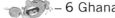

Serves: 12 – 6 Ghanaian fishermen

Prep Time: 20 minutes
Cooking Time: 10 minutes

- 1 large mango
- 1 lb (16oz) large shrimp, cleaned and peeled
- 1 tablespoon olive oil
- 1 teaspoon seasoned salt (or salt)
- 1 teaspoon black pepper
- 5 teaspoons butter
- 1 cup (8oz) grated mozzarella cheese
- 1 large yautia (or cocoyam)
- 1 large batata (or sweet potato)
- 1 medium yuca (or cassava)
- 1 medium potato
- 2 cups water

M.I.N.

Peel and cut yautia, potato, batata and yuca into small cubes. Place in a large pot over high heat; add water and boil for about 15 minutes, or until cooked and tender. Drain water.

Mash potato variety into a smooth, lump-free paste. Mix butter into paste for an even, smooth mix.

In a wok, stir fry shrimp with olive oil, seasoned salt and black pepper. Remove from fire when cooked.

Peel mango and cut into 2 – 3 inch flat pieces. Preheat oven grill.

Cut several 3-inch by 3-inch squares of foil. With a tablespoon, scoop mashed potato variety onto each piece of foil, flatten with a spoon. Sprinkle grated mozzarella on top to cover the individual surfaces completely.

Place in grill for about 3 – 5 minutes, or long enough for mozzarella to melt.

Take out of grill and let cool for 2 minutes. Top each with mango then one shrimp per piece.

Just serve this fruity finger delight.

Shrimp by Mango is a recipe which got its name before it came to life. I figured it sounds fancy, like a dress by a famous fashion designer. So this recipe is the only recipe I refer to as part of my designer collection. What? Well, not designer fashion wear but designer food from the "Tropical Ghana Delights" cookbook. I raved about the name, telling myself every morning about how fancy the name is and how great the recipe can be, and one morning it dawned on me what to do to make this happen. I did it. And the recipe is alive and kicking, just the way I envisioned it; something very different, special in its own way and a finger food that will make you rave.

Plantain Basil Cakes

Serves: 24

– a music band

Prep Time: 15 minutes
Baking Time: 30 minutes

Plantain Basil Cakes takes its root from Ghana and Mama Kate's plantain cake recipe. It uses the same techniques I learned growing up, but varies in ingredients. For instance, I have completely omitted flour, and I use breadcrumbs to give the recipe a more refined and rich taste. The basil is what actually makes this a very special finger food; it will change your perception of plantains and bananas once you try it. Let the Plantain Basil Cakes be your new food companion when you are serving friends or family at the dinner table. It is a finger food that will keep them asking questions and begging for more.

- 10 very ripe and soft plantains, peeled
- 2 scallions
- 8 tablespoons spiced palm oil (4 tablespoons olive oil)
- 20 fresh basil leaves
- 1 teaspoon salt
- 1½ teaspoons cayenne pepper
- 6 tablespoons freshly minced ginger root
- 1 clove garlic
- 1½ cup (12oz) breadcrumbs
- 1¼ cup (10oz) water

M.I.N.

Cut plantains into small pieces and divide into two parts. Add basil leaves, ginger root, garlic, scallions and some water to one part of plantain in blender and blend. Repeat process for remaining plantains.

Preheat oven to 450°F (232°C).

In a large bowl mix all blended plantains together; add cayenne pepper and spiced palm oil. Continue mixing by adding breadcrumbs gradually until you have a smooth, lump-free mixture.

Fill two loaf pans or 24 cupcake cases. Place in oven for 10 minutes, then reduce heat to 375°F (191°C) and let bake slowly, occasionally turning pans around. Bake 20 minutes (for cupcake cases) and 30 minutes (for loaf pans.)

Remove and let cool; cut loaves into 12 pieces each, and serve this plantain finger food.

Tip: Loaf Pan Trick!
Make sure to brush loaf pan with palm oil or olive oil.

Avocado Curry Slices V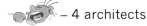

Serves: 8 – 4 architects

Prep Time: 20 minutes / Cooking Time: 10 minutes

Avocado Curry Slices is a concept that comes from an earlier idea, Sweet Potato Avocado Plate. This idea remained dormant until I had a conversation with my friend Win-Sie who is vegetarian. She mentioned that it would definitely be good to make sure to remember her and all other vegetarians when writing this book. And by seriously considering our conversation, the earlier dormant idea started to take shape. I encourage you to try this recipe even though you might not be a vegetarian. And if you are a vegetarian, I hope this touches you in a delightful way and satisfies your tropical craving.

- 2 avocados
- 1 ripe mango
- 2 medium carrots
- 4 teaspoons curry powder
- 3 crushed bay leaves
- 1 teaspoon seasoned salt (or salt)
- 1 teaspoon black pepper
- 2 tablespoons butter
- 1 teaspoon honey
- 1 large yautia (or cocoyam)
- 1 large batata (or sweet potato)
- 1 medium yuca (or cassava)
- 1 medium potato
- 2 cups water

M.I.N.

Peel and cut yautia, potato, batata and yuca into small cubes. Place in a large pot over high heat, add water and boil for about 15 – 20 minutes, or until cooked and tender. Drain water.

Mash potato variety into a smooth, lump-free mixture. Mix in butter. Add honey, seasoned salt, black pepper, crushed bay leaves and curry powder. Mix together for a smooth dark gold color.

Cut each avocado into quarters, discarding the seed and slightly peeling off the skin. Place on plate.

Put potato variety curry mix into a piping bag, and with your favorite tip, pipe curry mix on avocado slices.

Cut mango and carrots into 2-inch strips and arrange on top of avocado with curry mix. Serve this curry sensation as an appetizer or quick snack.

BELLY
FULL

Grilled Shrimp Mix, p. 26

Grilled Shrimp Mix

Serves: 5 — 3 hungry teenagers

Prep Time: 20 minutes / Cooking Time: 30 minutes

I love shrimp. One afternoon, I decided to fry fresh shrimp as I do most times to eat it with rice. As I placed my frying pan on the stove, it occurred to me that at one point in my life I enjoyed shrimp with some kind of tomato sauce my mother made. So I decided since I had some sun-dried tomatoes, I would add them to the shrimp and grill it instead. I was not too happy with the taste, but luckily I had some shrimp left! A few days later, I had a dream of what else to add to the recipe and found the perfect taste.

• 2 lbs (32oz) medium shrimp, cleaned and peeled

For Potato Variety

• 2 medium potatoes, peeled, cleaned and cut into quarters
• 3 medium batata (or sweet potatoes) peeled, cleaned and cut into quarters
• 2 medium yuca (or cassava) peeled, cleaned and cut into quarters
• 3 medium yautia (or cocoyam) peeled, cleaned and cut into quarters
• 2 cups (16oz) water

For Mix

• 1 tablespoon olive oil (or vegetable oil)
• 4 tablespoons mayonnaise
• 6 tablespoons finely chopped (or minced) sun-dried tomatoes
• 1 tangerine
• 4 teaspoons fresh minced ginger root
• 2 tablespoons worcestershire sauce
• 1½ teaspoons salt
• 1 teaspoon black pepper
• ½ teaspoon of cayenne pepper
• 2 teaspoons sugar
• ½ cup (4oz) water

M.I.N.

In a large pot, bring potatoes, sweet potatoes, cassava and cocoyam to boil with 2 cups water for 10 minutes over high heat.

In a small saucepan, combine sun-dried tomatoes, sugar and ½ cup of water. Stir continuously over medium heat for about 5 minutes. Let cool and add mayonnaise. Check on boiling potato variety and drain water.

In a wok, toss shrimp, olive oil, seasoned salt and black pepper over high heat for 3 minutes, or until shrimp turns orange.

Preheat oven grill.

Cut potato variety quarters into cubes, pour mayonnaise mix over and add shrimp. Sprinkle cayenne pepper over and mix. Sprinkle with tangerine juice, and pour onto aluminum foil covered baking sheet. Place in oven grill. Grill for about 10 – 15 minutes, turning mix over at least once with a turner, until grilled with tiny golden brown spots.

Belly fill your tummy by serving it hot, right off the grill.

Tangerine Handmade Bread V

Serves: 15 – 10 athletes

Prep Time: 35 minutes (Rising Time: 3 hours)
Baking Time: 25 minutes

Bread is one of the first foods I learned how to make. As the name implies, this is bread infused with tangerine and easily made at home. It is made just like any other bread with yeast and other ingredients, but it has a tropical feel to it that makes it very appetizing. Bread is something I just dip my fingers into flour and easily make. But the Tangerine Handmade Bread has undergone some changes that make it tangerine mouth-watering tasty. It's absolutely the bread you want to serve to convince anyone to believe in your bread making skills.

Tangerine Secret

- 6 large tangerines
- 1 teaspoon vanilla extract (or essence)
- ½ cup (4oz) milk
- 2 tablespoons brandy
- ½ cup (4oz) water

For Flour Mix

- 8½ cups (68oz) all purpose flour
- ¾ cup (6oz) margarine
- ½ cup (4oz) butter
- ¾ cup (6oz) raisins
- ½ cup (4oz) sugar
- 3 teaspoons salt
- 1½ teaspoons baking powder
- 2 tablespoons dry yeast
- ½ nutmeg, grated

M.I.N.

In a large bowl, mix flour, sugar, salt, raisins, baking powder and nutmeg. Mix in dry yeast. Make a hole in the flour mix, and add in margarine and butter.

Combine milk, brandy, vanilla extract and tangerine juice. Stir well, and pour it gradually into the hole with the margarine and butter.

Use hands to mix the tangerine solution into the flour, starting from the center hole, and working your way to the edge. Add water and continue mixing until your bread dough begins to form. Work the dough for about 5 minutes, tossing, turning and kneading with hands.

Cut dough to the size of an egg and form it into different shapes; place on a greased baking sheet tossed lightly with flour. Set in a warm place to rise.

Let rise for about 3 hours, or when the dough is twice its original size.

Preheat oven to 500°F (260°C). Brush top of dough with milk for a golden finish and place in oven.

After 5 minutes, turn heat to 400°F (204°C) and let bread bake for about 20 minutes, turning occasionally, until golden brown. Serve this finger food with butter or cheese spread.

Painted Fish +

Serves: 10 — 5 tailors

Prep Time: 15 minutes / Cooking Time: 20 minutes

I love painting. I have been painting since I was a kid, but I never made it to fame like the big name artists. This recipe came not too long after the Jumbo Fruity Shrimp came to life. I woke up one morning with a really weird dream of me painting a big fish with a brush. And as I snapped out of the dream, the first thing I said was "Lord, is this a career change for me?" I did not get an answer. A few weeks later, my answer came, and here we are today with the Painted Fish recipe. It's fun to paint and cook; try it out, remembering the days you started playing with colors and making a mess everywhere. This time around, though, you are going to use that technique to fill your belly with food.

• 2 large white or red snapper, scaled and cut into 5 pieces each

First Coat Paint
• 3 tablespoons condensed milk
• 1 lemon

Finishing Coat Paint
• 1 large tangerine
• 4 tablespoons steamed rice
• ¼ sweet pineapple
• 2 tablespoons pineapple jam (or marmalade)
• 2 tablespoons evaporated milk

M.I.N.

Add fresh lemon juice to condensed milk, mix well and coat fish completely using a brush. Let dry for 5 minutes.

Turn on oven grill.

Combine tangerine juice, rice and pineapple in a blender. Blend into a smoothie. Add pineapple jam and evaporated milk, and mix well.

With a brush, paint fish with finishing coat mix and grill. Keep brushing with more paint as needed, turning occasionally on grill until golden and cooked.

Serve this fish to belly fill your tummy.

Tip: Paint Salmon!
Use salmon instead for a tasty painted fish and top with chocolate syrup for a delicious meal.

Ghana Style Jollof Rice Remixed

Serves: 4  – 2 starving artists

Prep Time: 90 minutes / Cooking Time: 30 minutes

For Special Gravy

- 3 tablespoons vegetable oil
- ½ cup (4oz) water
- 1 teaspoon white pepper
- 2 teaspoons salt
- 1 teaspoon curry powder
- 1 tablespoon worcestershire sauce
- 1 tablespoon minced ginger
- 1 tablespoon minced garlic
- 5 tablespoons fresh finely chopped basil
- 4 large ripe tomatoes
- 2 scallions (or spring onions)
- 1 small red onion
- 6 tablespoons tomato paste (or puree)

For Rice

- 2 cups (16oz) long grain rice
- 2½ cups (20oz) water
- 1 teaspoon salt

For Remix

- 1 tablespoon butter
- 1 lb (16oz) medium shrimp, cleaned and peeled
- 1 teaspoon black pepper
- 1 teaspoon seasoned salt (or salt)
- ¾ cup (6oz) chopped carrots
- 3 tablespoons fresh finely chopped basil

M.I.N.

In a large pot combine oil, ginger and garlic over medium heat.

Peel and clean onions, and blend together in a blender with part of water. Add to sizzling garlic and ginger, and turn heat to high. Add tomato paste, and stir continuously for about 5 minutes.

Add basil and continue stirring for about 7 – 10 minutes.

Blend fresh tomatoes with rest of water and add to gravy mix. Continue stirring for about 5 minutes. Partly cover with lid and let boil, stirring occasionally for gravy to cook – about 15 minutes.

Reduce heat to low and let boil gently for another 15 minutes, still stirring occasionally.

Wash rice twice to reduce the starch content, and add to boiling gravy. Stir rice and increase heat to medium. Continue to stir frequently (to prevent rice from sticking to bottom of pot) until almost all gravy liquid is absorbed.

Add 2½ cups of water and salt, and increase heat to high. Let boil and occasionally stir till all the water is almost absorbed by the rice. Reduce heat to low.

Spread aluminum foil to cover top of pot and place lid on top to trap steam. Allow rice to cook completely for about 15 – 20 minutes (or until completely tender and well cooked).

As you wait for rice to cook, combine shrimp, butter, black pepper and seasoned salt in a wok over high heat until shrimp is stir fried – about 5 minutes.

When rice is cooked, mix with shrimp and carrots in the wok. Sprinkle fresh basil on top and fill your belly.

Jollof rice is very popular in Ghana and some West African countries like Nigeria, Senegal, Gambia and Sierra Leone. When I started working on this book and decided to find out why it is so popular, I found out that "Jollof" rice was actually "Wolof" rice, which was a popular dish in the Wolof tribe of West Africa, before the demarcation of borders. With the spread of people all over, I am not surprised that there are varying versions of this recipe. However, I wanted to remix it my way, the way my mother taught me to cook while growing up in Ghana. Hence the name! It is a remix of what existed long before I was born. It is a very special version that's different from all the rest and will really fill your belly full.

ICE CREAM
SOCIALS

Beer Mango Extraordinaire, p. 33

Beer Mango Fruit Harvest V

Serves: 20  – 15 soccer mums

Prep Time: 20 minutes
Cooking Time: 35 minutes

I am not a beer drinker; the best I will do is to sample it by mixing it with coke or ginger ale to make what I grew to know as "Shandy." So as a beer "non-lover," I found another way to use this drink that some people absolutely love. As I explored ways to use beer, it occurred to me that beer and mango might be the answer. As a kid in Ghana, I grew up with mango trees (some as old as me), and my love for this fruit has never stopped. So I figured I would combine beer for people in my close circle who love it so much with my great love for mangoes by harvesting both ingredients in the same basket. After several trials and errors, this recipe was born, bringing out beer and mango in a delightful way.

- 6 cups (48oz) all purpose flour
- ¼ cup (2oz) butter
- ¼ cup (2oz) margarine
- ½ cup (4oz) sugar
- 1 cup (8oz) raisins
- 1 teaspoon baking powder
- 6 tangerines
- 1 lemon
- 2 large finely chopped ripe mangoes
- ½ cup (4oz) water
- 1 bottle 12 fl oz (355ml) chilled
Heineken beer (Club or your favorite beer)

- 1 teaspoon vanilla extract (or essence)

M.I.N.

Preheat oven to 450 °F (232 °C).

In a large bowl, combine flour, sugar, margarine, butter and baking powder. Mix completely. Add raisins and mangoes, and grate in lemon rind. Continue mixing. Halve tangerines and lemon, and add juice to mix. Add vanilla extract to beer, and stir beer gradually into flour mix. Add water and mix batter completely.

Pour batter onto two flat greased baking sheets (or one large greased baking sheet); level with a spatula and place in oven. After 10 minutes, reduce oven to 400 °F (204 °C); let bake for another 15 – 20 minutes, or until lightly brown.

Take out of oven, let cool, cut into squares and top with chocolate syrup. Make this an ice cream social by serving with your favorite ice cream, hot chocolate, coffee or tea.

Beer Mango Fruit Extrordinaire +

Serves: 12 – 6 construction workers

Prep Time: 20 minutes
Cooking Time: 30 minutes

- 6 cups (48oz) all purpose flour
- ¼ cup (2oz) butter
- ¼ cup (2oz) margarine
- ½ cup (4oz) sugar
- 1 cup (8oz) raisins
- 1 teaspoon baking powder
- 8 tangerines
- 1 lemon
- 3 large finely chopped ripe mangoes
- ¾ cup (6oz) water
- 1 bottle 12 fl oz (532 ml) chilled beer (your favorite)
- 1 teaspoon vanilla extract (essence)
- 3 tablespoons vegetable oil
- 1 sachet Bird's custard mix or your favorite pudding mix

M.I.N.

In a large bowl, combine flour, sugar, margarine, butter and baking powder. Mix completely. Add raisins, 2 chopped mangoes and grate in lemon rind. Continue mixing. Halve tangerines and lemon, and add juice to mix. Add vanilla extract to beer, and stir mixture gradually into flour mix. Add water and mix batter completely.

Cover batter with dump cloth, and let sit for 10 minutes

Uncover batter and stir. Heat frying pan and put a teaspoon of oil in the pan over medium heat.

Fill frying pan with 2 ladles full of batter. Let cook slowly until batter solidifies and turns light brown. Use a slotted turner to flip and fry till light brown.

Make about 8 Beer Mango Fruit pancakes.

Prepare Bird's custard mix by adding a little red or pink food color (or your favorite color) – do the same for your favorite pudding mix. Make several layers of Beer Mango Fruit pancakes and pudding by mounting on top of each other with pudding in between pancake layers.

On the last layer, place a little pudding on top and sprinkle the rest of chopped mango, evenly covering the final layer. Serve this extraordinaire delight as is or with ice cream, and you are good to go.

Tip: Use A Waffle Maker!
Use a waffle maker to create different shapes instead of pan frying.

Beer Mango Fruit Extraordinaire comes from Beer Mango Fruit Harvest, and it is also known to me as Beer Mango Fruit Harvest 2°. This just means it has much more delight for your enjoyment. Compared to the original, it has more mango, it's pan-fried instead of baked and it is layered with your favorite pudding mix. This recipe might send you daydreaming in wonderland, so make it a treat for yourself or surprise your guest. It will make most people who forget easily remember your name, even if you were just introduced to them. Should you make this recipe, you might see your party grow bigger than the list of invited people (think: party crashers).

Cocoa Bars

Serves: 30 — 15 scouts

Prep Time: 15 minutes / Cooking Time: 35 minutes

Cocoa Bars is a recipe that's special to me because cocoa reminds me of growing up and enjoying Ghana cocoa (sucking on the fresh seeds from the pod). The cocoa pod, which is green, turns golden when it ripens. When green, it reminds me of freshness and fresh vegetation; the golden color just shows its richness. Using 100% cocoa from Ghana for the recipe just makes it fresh, rich and special. The mixture of fruit and oats gives it a texture that is different and amazing at the same time. It smells like chocolate and looks like a brownie but do not be deceived; it is different and special. This is definitely a delicacy you cannot resist.

- ¾ sweet pineapple, blended
- 1 orange
- 4 tangerines
- 1 lemon
- 3 eggs
- ½ cup (4oz) bread crumbs
- 5 tablespoons of unsweetened natural cocoa (or cacao) powder
- 4 tablespoons brandy
- 3 tablespoons honey
- 2 14oz (396g) cans condensed milk
- 2 teaspoons vanilla extract (or essence)
- 5 cups (40oz) Quaker oats
- 1 teaspoon baking powder
- 1½ cups (12oz) raisins
- 2 tablespoons all purpose flour

Optional Add-In

1 cup (8oz) roasted cashews, crushed

M.I.N.

Combine condensed milk and cocoa powder in a large bowl. Mix well to remove all lumps. Add blended pineapple, orange and tangerine juices and continue mixing.

Preheat oven to 500°F (260°C).

In a separate bowl, whisk eggs and add to mixture.

Add lemon rind and juice, honey, brandy and vanilla extract. Mix together, then stir in oats, bread crumbs and baking powder.

Toss raisins with flour, add to mixture and mix well.

Add optional cashews at this stage and continue to mix.

Pour mix onto two flat greased baking sheets and level with spatula. Place in oven and after 5 minutes reduce heat to 400°F (204°C).

Let bake for 20 minutes, turning baking sheets around occasionally. Remove when mixture solidifies and is firm. Let cool. Cut into 30 cubes or rectangles. Serve with coffee or ice cream.

Tropical Ghana Splash

Tropical Ghana Splash is a drink made with fresh tangerine, coconut water, mango and pineapple juices. But it changes as you add different ingredients to boost the flavor. This boost is known as the Splash. So when you add a new ingredient, like fresh grapefruit juice, you create a Splash. Or when you add soursop, you create a different Splash. Try a Splash with any of the listed ingredients below. Add your favorite ingredients, too. Explore your own Splash and share if you want. Splash your life with a new flavor.

SPLASH BASIC (Serves 4)

5 fresh sweet tangerines (juiced)
2 cups (16oz) fresh coconut water
1 sweet pineapple (peeled and chopped)
2 large ripe mangos (peeled and chopped)

Combine all ingredients in a blender to create a smoothie with your favorite one (1) two (2) or three (3) Splash boosters below.

TRY TO USE FRESH INGREDIENTS ONLY.
PRESERVED VARIETIES WILL NOT GIVE YOU A SPLASH!

Guanabana (Soursop)
Grapefruit
Guava
Papaya (Pawpaw)
Passion Fruit
Sugar Apple (Custard Apple / Sweetsop)

All fruits with seeds should be seeded before creating a SPLASH.

Mix & Match Tips

You can combine, mix and match in any way you like for your love interest or guests.

Amazing 5

Wins over your stubborn future in-laws
(1-On A Light Note + 2-Finger Foods + 1-Belly Full + 1-Ice Cream Social)

- ~ Grandmama Light Soup, p. 9
- ~ Honey Green Chicken, p. 11
- ~ Plantain Boats, p. 14
- ~ Grilled Shrimp Mix, p. 26
- ~ Beer Mango Fruit Harvest, p. 32

Happy 4ever

Leaves your employees thinking... quitting is a bad idea
(3-Finger Foods + 1-Ice Cream Social)

- ~ Honey Green Chicken, p. 11
- ~ Avocado Curry Slices, 24
- ~ Tropical Mini Pies, p. 20
- ~ Cocoa Bars, p. 35

I Love U

Just to encourage him or her to think of committing...
(3-Finger Foods)

- ~ Honey Green Chicken, p. 11
- ~ Shrimp by Mango, p. 22
- ~ Plantain Boats, p. 14

All Out

Keeping cocktails alive and kicking
(8-Finger Foods + 1-Belly Full + Tropical Ghana Splash + 1-Ice Cream Social)

- ~ Tropical Mini Pies, p. 20 / Plantain Mama, p. 15
- ~ Egg Plates, p. 17 / Mackerel Tarts, p.12
- ~ Bacon Basil Wrap, p. 16 / Avocado Curry Slices, p. 24
- ~ Honey Green Chicken, p. 11 / Tangerine Handmade Bread, p. 27
- ~ Cocoa Bars, p. 35 / Tangerine Ginger Chicken, p. 18
- ~ Tropical Ghana Splash, p. 36

Index

ABOUT THE AUTHOR

Charles A. Cann's love and joy for food and cooking is what led him to start the Tropical Ghana Cookbook series with his first cookbook, "Tropical Ghana Delights." As he works on his next cookbook, "Tropical Ghana Inspirations," he hopes the first will give food lovers a way to enjoy Ghanaian cuisine in a refreshing way. Charles, or the Tropical Ghana Chef as he is known in the kitchen, explores new ways of contemporary Ghanaian cooking by fusing traditional and non-traditional Ghanaian cooking techniques. In doing this, he uses this book to highlight a less celebrated side of Ghanaian cooking – hors d'oeuvres.

Part of the proceeds of the Tropical Ghana Cookbook series will go to the Tropical Ghana Spirit fund, which Charles set up to help and provide food for less privileged children in Ghana with a focus on education. Cann's idea is that as people enjoy the recipes in this cookbook, they are also encouraging a child in Ghana to stay in school by nourishing youth with meals that will help them remain focused on achieving their goals. By buying this book and enjoying the recipes, you are also helping to place a smile on a child's face in Ghana. Visit the cookbook website www.tropicalghanacookbooks.com to learn more.